LA GRANGE
PUBLIC LIBRARY

10 West Cossitt Avenue
La Grange, IL 60525
lagrangelibrary.org   708.215.3200

This library edition published in 2012 by Walter Foster Publishing, Inc.
Distributed by Black Rabbit Books.
P.O. Box 3263 Mankato, Minnesota 56002

Designed and published by Walter Foster Publishing, Inc.
Walter Foster is a registered trademark.

Printed in Mankato, Minnesota, USA by CG Book Printers, a division of Corporate Graphics.

First Library Edition

Library of Congress Cataloging-in-Publication Data

Watch me draw Diego's animal adventures / illustrated by Susan Hall. --
1st Library Edition
       pages cm
  ISBN 978-1-936309-88-7
 1. Animals in art--Juvenile literature. 2. Cartoon
characters--Juvenile literature. 3. Drawing--Technique--Juvenile
literature. 4. Go, Diego, go! (Television program)--Juvenile literature.
 I. Hall, Susan T., 1940- illustrator. II. Title: Diego's animal
adventures.
  NC1764.8.A54W38 2012
  741.5'1--dc23
                          2012004012

052012
17679

9 8 7 6 5 4 3 2 1

NOV 2013

$17.95

WATCH ME DRAW

DIEGO'S ANIMAL ADVENTURES

Illustrated by Susan Hall

¡Hola! I'm Diego and this is my older sister, Alicia. We're Animal Scientists. Whenever we help an animal friend, we learn more about animals. Like when we helped Mommy Macaw, we learned that scarlet macaws eat bananas and other tropical forest fruits.

Draw the scarlet macaw!

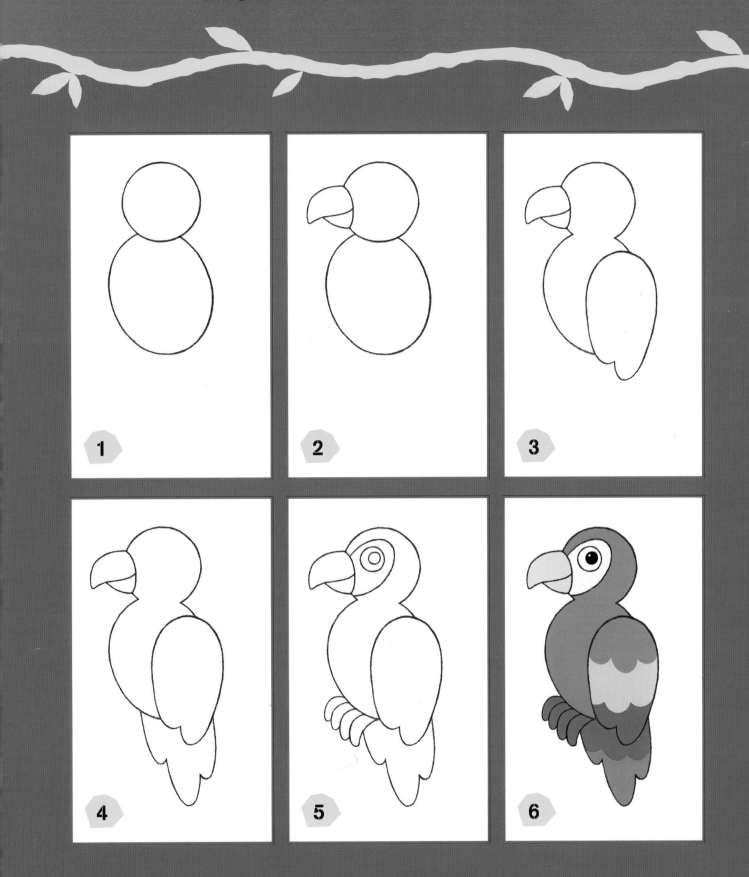

Red-eyed tree frogs
have really sticky toes to
help them climb trees!
They live in trees!

Draw the red-eyed tree frog!

When we helped Chinta the Chinchilla find her way home, we found out that chinchillas can hop really high! Hop, hop!

Draw the chinchilla!

Armadillos can roll themselves into a ball for protection! They're really great diggers too!

Draw the three-banded armadillo!

Our friend Sammy the Sloth lives in the trees in the rain forest! Sloths like to hang upside down from branches.

Draw the three-toed sloth!

My cousin Dora helped me when we needed to find a lost wolf pup. Maned wolves have long legs, which make it easier for them to raise up high to see over the tall grasses.

Draw the maned wolf!

We learned about emperor penguins when we went to study penguins in Antarctica! Emperor penguins are the biggest penguins in the world!

Draw the emperor penguin!

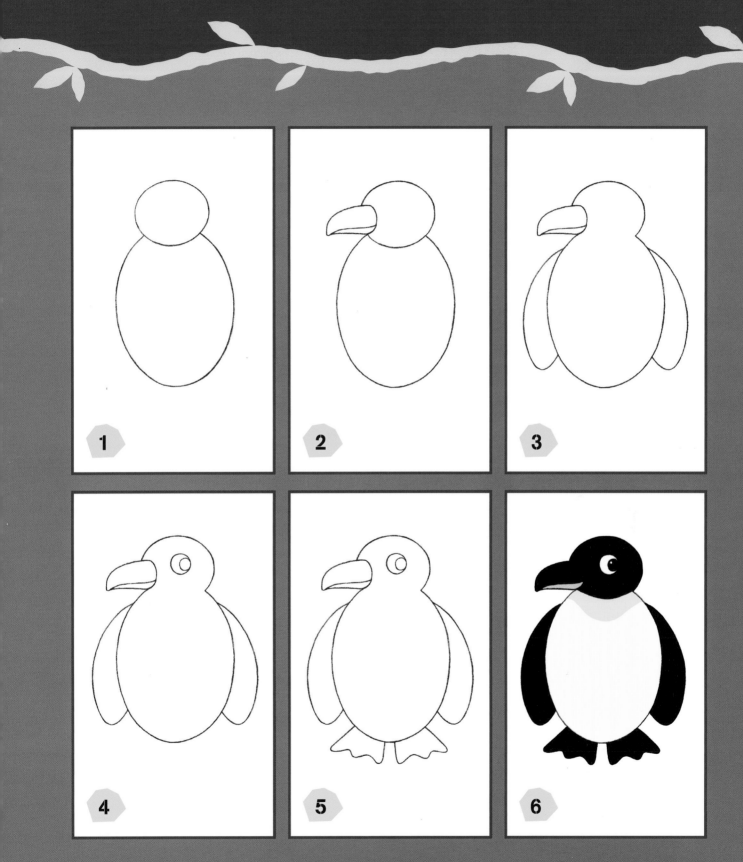

Anacondas are great swimmers, and they spend
a lot of time in water so they don't dry out!

Draw the anaconda!

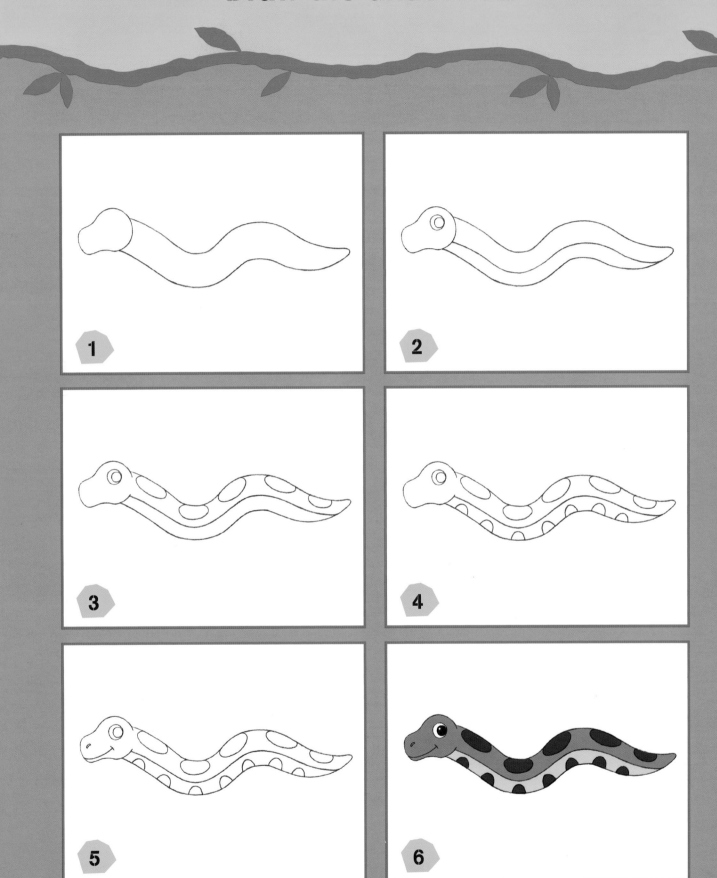

We help animals in the ocean too, like humpback whales. Humpback whales get their name from the way their backs bend as they swim!

Draw the humpback whale!

Llamas like my friend Linda sure are great climbers! That's a good thing, too, because they live high in the mountains.

Draw the llama!

When we helped my friend Tuga, we learned more about leatherback sea turtles. They are the largest living turtle in the world!

Draw the leatherback sea turtle!

Thanks for helping us learn
so much about animals!
You're a great Animal
Scientist too!